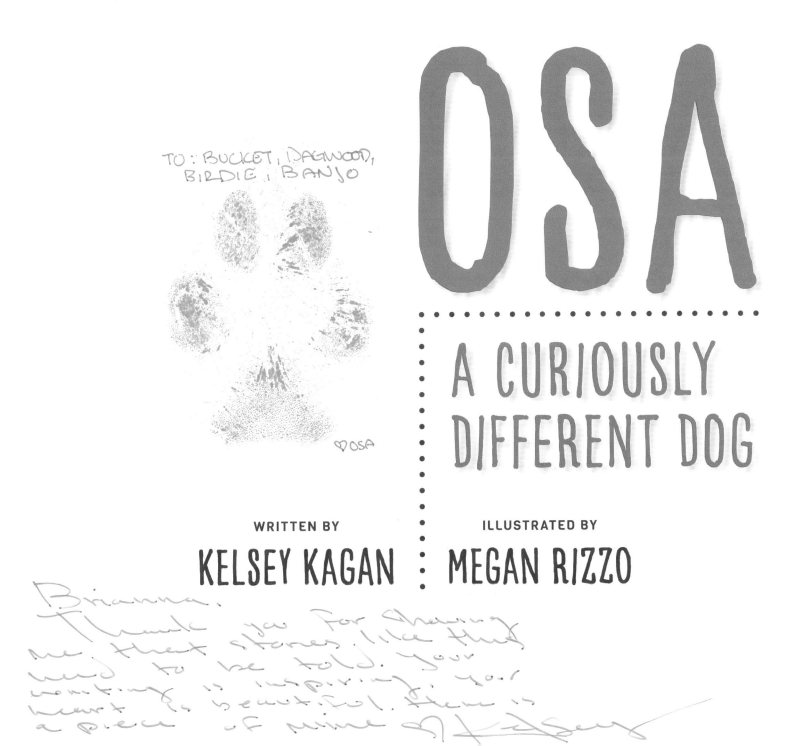

TO : BUCKET, DAGWOOD,
BIRDIE, BANJO

♡ OSA

OSA

A CURIOUSLY DIFFERENT DOG

WRITTEN BY

KELSEY KAGAN

ILLUSTRATED BY

MEGAN RIZZO

Brianna,
Thank you for showing
me that stories like this
need to be told. Your
writing is inspiring. Your
heart is beautiful. Here is
a piece of mine ♡ Kelsey

ISBN: 978-0-9962282-2-0
Library of Congress Control Number: 2020948266
©2021 by Arnica Creative Services

Author: Kelsey Kagan
Illustrations © 2021 by Megan Rizzo
Printed in the U.S.A. All rights reserved

Book Cover Design: Aimee Genter-Gilmore
Cover art: Megan Rizzo
Book Interior Layout: Aimee Genter-Gilmore
Editor-in-Chief: Gloria Martinez
Publisher: Ross Hawkins

ACS, LLC
Portland, Oregon | Palm Desert, California
Ideasbyacs.com

A portion of the proceeds from book sales of *Osa: A Curiously Different Dog* will be donated to animal rescue organizations.

DEDICATION

To Osa, the curiously different dog who inspired this book, and inspires me every day, and to all the other dogs, people, and creatures of the world who feel like misfits. You fit, dear ones, you fit.

—KELSEY KAGAN

ACKNOWLEDGMENTS

To Ry, my partner in life and all things, who tells me I am great so emphatically I am forced to believe it.

To my sister, Katie, who taught me, among a million other lessons, that loving a dog will bring rewards beyond anything imaginable, and my brother Robbie, who tolerates the pups we bring around him. And to my parents, who encouraged this child to always stay wild.

To the friends that see uniqueness as something to rejoice in and create a space of welcoming love. I'm so blessed that we found our way to each other.

To my nieces and nephews, a list ever growing as my friends continue to bring new, wonderful life into this world. You were on my mind while I wrote every word.

Gloria, Ross, Aimee, and Megan—what a team. You all made my dreams come true, and I will thank you in my heart every day for what you have given me.

Alexis, your guidance brought meaning to this book, and Rachel, your efforts ensure that dogs everywhere will receive the help they deserve.

To my readers, for choosing a book that celebrates love and acceptance, of ourselves and one another.

1

On a sunny Saturday in May, Osa was digging for bones when her brother Jasper came screeching into the yard.

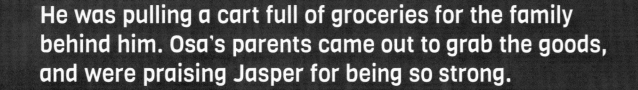

He was pulling a cart full of groceries for the family behind him. Osa's parents came out to grab the goods, and were praising Jasper for being so strong.

"Why don't they ever have *me* pull the cart?" Osa asked.

"I am an Alaskan Malamute, sis." Jasper responded. "I am built to pull heavy weights over long distances. You can tell by my thick shoulders and wide chest."

4

As they went into the house, Osa thought about that. She wasn't sure what she was born to do. She looked at her brother with his big, strong body and caught her own reflection in the oven door.

She didn't look like her brother. Come to think about it, she didn't look like her friends either. She didn't look like ANY DOG she had ever seen!

Osa walked down the trail behind her house where she bumped into her good friend, Wilber the cat.

"Hey, happy dog!" Wilber shouted from his perch.
"You don't look as happy as usual,
is everything okay?"

"I'm having a hard time figuring out who I am and *what* I am.
I don't look like any of my friends."

"Some of their ears point up towards the sky. My ears flop down towards the ground.

"Some of their hair is twisty and curly, like the tip of a piggy's tail. My hair is straight as an arrow.

"Some of their eyes are golden or brown. My eyes are blue as a bottomless lake."

"I'm going to ask around to see what I can learn."

"Well then, I'm coming with you!" said Wilber, "I can help you, and besides that... *everything* is better with friends!"

The pair spotted their friend, Maggie, just down the road. Maggie is a sweet dog with long, luxurious hair.

"I wonder if you and Osa are the same, you both have such lovely hair!" Wilber exclaimed.

"I'm an Irish Setter," said Maggie, as she shook her beautiful mane. "You have red in your hair, just like mine! It's really beautiful when it catches the light, isn't it? It looks just like a summer sunrise."

"You both have the best hair on the block," Wilber declared, "but I think there's more to being an Irish Setter than great hair."

"He's right! We have slender legs, big bushy tails, and excellent noses. All of these things make us magnificent bird hunters."

Just then they heard a loud, familiar bark.

"There's Colt! He has a very big bark that helps him protect the neighborhood," Wilber explained. "Osa, you protect your people and keep them safe, maybe you two are the same!"

"I am a German Shepherd, I use my big *WOOF!* to warn everyone of any mischief," said Colt. "Try letting out a big bark, let's see what you've got!"

Osa barked a tiny little *woof!*

"Well Osa, your bark may not be as big as Colt's, but it's still a very good bark and your family is lucky to have you guarding them," said Wilber.

"He's right, Osa," Colt interjected. "Big or little, a bark is a bark, and you are very brave."

"Hey Ruby, where ya' headed?!" Osa called out when she saw her friend walking down the road with a bundle of baskets.

"I'm headed to the beach, gotta get things ready for the annual picnic!" Ruby said with a little *arf!* as she sauntered away.

"Osa, you and Ruby are both the most helpful dogs in town, maybe you two are the same," Wilber thought out loud.

The pair caught up to Ruby and asked her if she could tell them more about herself.

"Well, I'm a Dalmatian, of course!"

"Could I possibly be one too?" Osa asked.

"Dalmatians hang around with firefighters, they have a ruff! job and we make their job easier."

"If the only requirement of being a Dalmatian is to be friendly and helpful, then I'd say perhaps you are," said Ruby. "But, I think there might be more to it than that."

They carried the picnic baskets to the beach and said their goodbyes.

BEACH

Suddenly, they heard a
roaring of hooves.

Blue came running toward
them, chasing a group of sheep
galloping across the field.

"Now there's someone who is just your speed,"
said Wilber as he dusted the dirt off his orange fur.

"Osa, my friend!" Blue shouted from behind a sheep, "I am an Australian Shepherd, but that doesn't mean I have to live in Australia. Being a shepherd means that I LOVE to herd! It's right there in my name. You might not be the same type of dog as me, but I know you love to chase and that's ALL I look for in a friend.

Come, chase things with me!"

Osa and Wilber got very hungry after all the running so they parted ways with Blue and his herd and went to find some food.

"Smells like Honey is baking up something splendid," Wilber said.

"Mmmm... yes, she is," Osa replied, nose high in the air sniffing the good smells.

"I wonder... If Honey likes to cook and I like to eat, do you think we could be the same?"

"Only one way to find out!" Said Wilber.

"Wilber, Osa, you two look mighty hungry," Honey said as she piled cookies high atop a big, shiny plate. "How have you worked up such an appetite?"

"We've been running and playing with our friends all day. I'm trying to learn more about who I am, and I've been asking my friends for help along the way."

"That's the best way to do it!" Honey said, stacking up even more cookies. "I'm a Great Dane, and you are a great friend and really great customer, that's for sure.

"We Great Danes are known for being GIANTS. If you ever need something from the top shelf, give a Great Dane a call!"

With plates full of cookies Wilber and Osa started back toward their homes.

"I don't get it," said Osa. "All of these friends and so many things are the same, but I'm still... *different* than all the others."

"Maybe that's the key, maybe being different is exactly what you should be," Wilber explained. "It's almost picnic time. I'll meet you there, happy dog!"

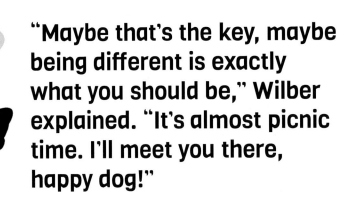

When Osa got home, Jasper was playing in the yard.

"What's up sister? Where have you been? What have you been up to?" Jasper asked.

"Wilber and I were out talking to our friends. You see, I'm trying to figure out why I am not the same as everyone else. Some friends have longer hair, some have bigger barks. Some dogs like to run really fast, and others like to lie around all day. Some are big and some are small."

"So you're telling me that you don't think we are the same just because we look a little different, or sound a little different, or like different things? That's really, *really* silly!"

"We are all **SO** *different.* None of us are the same." Osa replied.

"What's the matter with that?" Jasper asked as they approached the beach. "Look around you, sister. Just look around!

"We are all more similar than we are different. See?"

"Toes and tails,
ears and nails,

Bellies full of laughs and ...
bodies full of wiggles!

Fur from the tops of our heads to
the bottom of our toes

and ... HAPPY tongues!"

23

"We run, we play...we laugh, all the same.

We bark and howl and whine and woof.

We listen to our parents ... most of the time.

We chase critters!

24

We eat cookies,
We laugh with our WHOLE bellies!

And we love each other with our WHOLE hearts!

These differences are the things that make us unique.

Besides, if everything and all of us
were exactly the same that would
be utterly boring!"

Osa thought about that for a while.

"You're right! I *AM* Osa.
I am a dog made up of many breeds.
My ears are floppy and my eyes are
blue. I like to lay in the sun and play and
have fun. I have a little bit of this and a
little of that. But most of all... I have a
lot of ME!

"There are things that make me
different, and that is very special. There
are so many things that make us all the
same, and that makes us family.

"*I am OSA!*
And that is the best thing for me to be."

And together with all of her friends,
Osa howled at the moon,
just like good dogs do.

THE REAL OSA

The author shares her personal story of pet adoption, the day she met the real Osa.

OLIVIA ASHTON PHOTOGRAPHY

A moment passed, then the small-framed dog slinked her way toward me. Her glacier eyes considered me once more, then she climbed into my lap, turned her head, and gave me the first of what would be one million big, sloppy kisses.

I adopted her that day.

Osa had had a few years of life before she met me, including multiple shelters and other families, but she was always my dog, and now she was finally home.

She's been trotting happily by my side, ears flopping and tail wagging, ever since.

I was volunteering as a dog walker at the Oregon Humane Society when a set of ice-blue eyes caught mine as I walked down the aisle of enclosures.

The card next to the door stated that this sweet gal was from the Second Chance Program, and had been adopted and returned once already. She was cowering in the back corner, her ears drooping sweetly beside her head, but her eyes were fixated on me. I couldn't tell if the steely stare was warning me to stay away, or inviting me in. I hoped it was the latter, and I slipped my master key into the padlock and carefully pushed the door open.

Slow as can be, I shimmied my body into the enclosure and sat on the ground in the opposite corner.

FACT:

OVER *SIX MILLION* COMPANION ANIMALS ENTER SHELTERS EACH YEAR.

ABOUT PET ADOPTION

Do you love dogs? Great! We do too. Here are some wonderful ways to help doggies in need:

GET INVOLVED: Volunteer programs are available at many levels. There are many ways to help, and the needs of shelters are ever changing, so connect with one near you to see how you can get involved.

DONATE: Start a dog food and treat drive in your community. Blankets, towels, and bedding are items often needed at shelters. Money donations are very helpful. Perhaps you could host a lemonade stand and give the profits to your local shelter. Shelter pets celebrate holidays just like you, and your family. Another idea is to host a toy drive and bring all of the toys to the animals for holiday gifts. Can you think of other ways to raise money for your local shelter?

ATTEND AN EVENT: Shelters host dozens of fundraising events in the communities they serve. Fun runs, photo contests, and more. As a bonus, they usually bring along cute doggies to play with! Check their calendars to find one in your area.

FORM A CLUB: Ask your teachers at school if you are allowed to form a club to help animals. You can host small events during lunch hours to share your passion with fellow students, and speak to other clubs or classes about animal welfare.

LEND A HAND: Does someone you know have a dog that they love dearly, but could use a helping hand? Maybe the dog owner has an injury, just had a new baby, or is elderly and getting their pup out for a walk every day is hard for them. With your parents' permission, ask if you could offer to take their dog out after school.

CLASS PRESENTATIONS: Ask your parents to help you schedule a speaker from a local shelter to talk to your class or club about animal care and talk about ways to be a good pet owner, and provide educational material about pet adoption.

BIRTHDAY PARTY FUNDRAISING: Instead of traditional gifts, ask friends for donations to the local shelter for your birthday party.

FOSTER: Foster volunteers provide temporary care for animals by bringing them into their own homes. Some animals don't thrive in the shelter environment and foster homes help animals with special needs, and gives them a less stressful environment so their personalities can shine through. Fostering is an amazing way to open your heart to an animal companion, and to see how a pet fits into your life.

ADOPT: adding an animal companion to the family is a huge commitment.

Before considering taking this big step, be honest about how much time you have to provide proper training and exercise, and think about the financial obligations.

WHAT IS A SHELTER?

An animal shelter is a place where animals are taken care of, fed, and kept safe while they wait for their permanent homes.

WHY DO ANIMALS ENTER SHELTERS?
An owner may make the tough decision to surrender their pet, or the animal may have been from a different shelter that couldn't care for them.

Some reasons an owner may surrender their animal are:

- Moving out of the area, or into a different home
- Their landlord changes rental agreement to not allow animals
- The animal may be incompatible with other pets
- A new job might make them too busy to give them proper attention
- They may develop health issues
- Veterinary bills may be too much of a financial burden